WHAT'S THE DIFFERENCE?
DAY AND NIGHT

Heather Amery
Illustrated by Peter Firmin

Consultant: Betty Root
Centre for the Teaching of Reading
University of Reading, England

Morning on the farm

The animals are having their breakfasts.
The cows have been milked and are going to the fields.

Evening on the farm

The animals are going to bed for the night. What are the children doing?

Morning in the street

The people are going to work.
The shopkeepers are very busy.

Evening in the street

The people are going home from work.
The shops are closing for the night.

Morning in the bedroom

It is time for the children to get up.
What are they doing?

Evening in the bedroom

It is time for the children to go to bed.
What are they doing now?

Morning in the kitchen

Everyone is having breakfast.
Who has to get dressed?

Evening in the kitchen

Everyone is having their supper.
Who has already gone to bed?

Morning in the house

It is time to go to school.
Everyone is clean and tidy.

Evening in the house

All the children are home from school.
What are they doing?

Morning at the campsite

There is lots of work to do before breakfast. Who has not got up yet?

Evening at the campsite

The grown-ups are having a barbecue supper. Where are all the children?

Daytime in the hospital

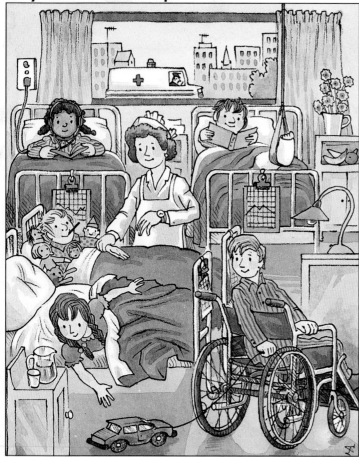

The children have had breakfast.
They are enjoying themselves.

Night-time in the hospital

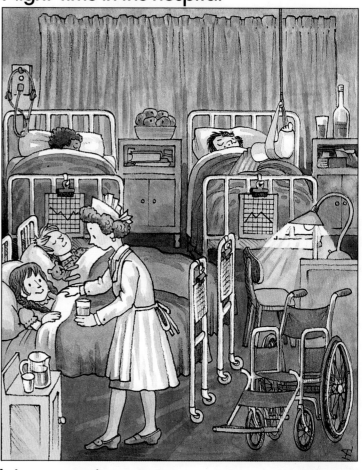

It is very quiet now.
Who is still awake?

Daytime in the harbour

The fishing boats have just come in.
There are lots of fish to unload.

Night-time in the harbour

The fishing boats are setting off.
Where do you think they are going?

Day in the café

It is very bright and busy.
Everyone is hungry.

Night in the café

The café is closed for the night.
There is lots of clearing up to do.

Day in the pet shop.

There are lots of animals to buy.
How many different ones can you see?

Night in the pet shop.

Most of the animals are asleep.
Which ones are still awake?

Day in the street

What are all the people doing? How many children can you count?

Night in the street

Most people have gone home to bed. But some people have to work at night.

Puzzle picture

Would you see these things in the morning, during the day or at night?

First published in 1985. Usborne Publishing Ltd, 20 Garrick Street, London WC2E 9BJ, England. ©Usborne Publishing Ltd. 1985

The name Usborne and the device 🎈 are Trade Marks of Usborne Publishing Ltd.

Printed in Portugal.